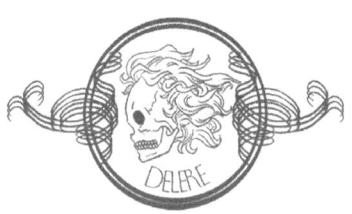

This paperback edition
first published in 2018 by Delere Press LLP

Text
© Jeremy Fernando;
Illustrations and cover design
© Natalie Christian Tan

***

First published in 2018 by Delere Press LLP
370G Alexandra Road, #09-09
Singapore 159960
www.delerepress.com
Delere Press LLP Reg No. T11LL1061K

All rights reserved.

ISBN 978-981-11-8442-0

resisting art
by Jeremy Fernando
alongside illustrations by Natalie Christian Tan

resisting art

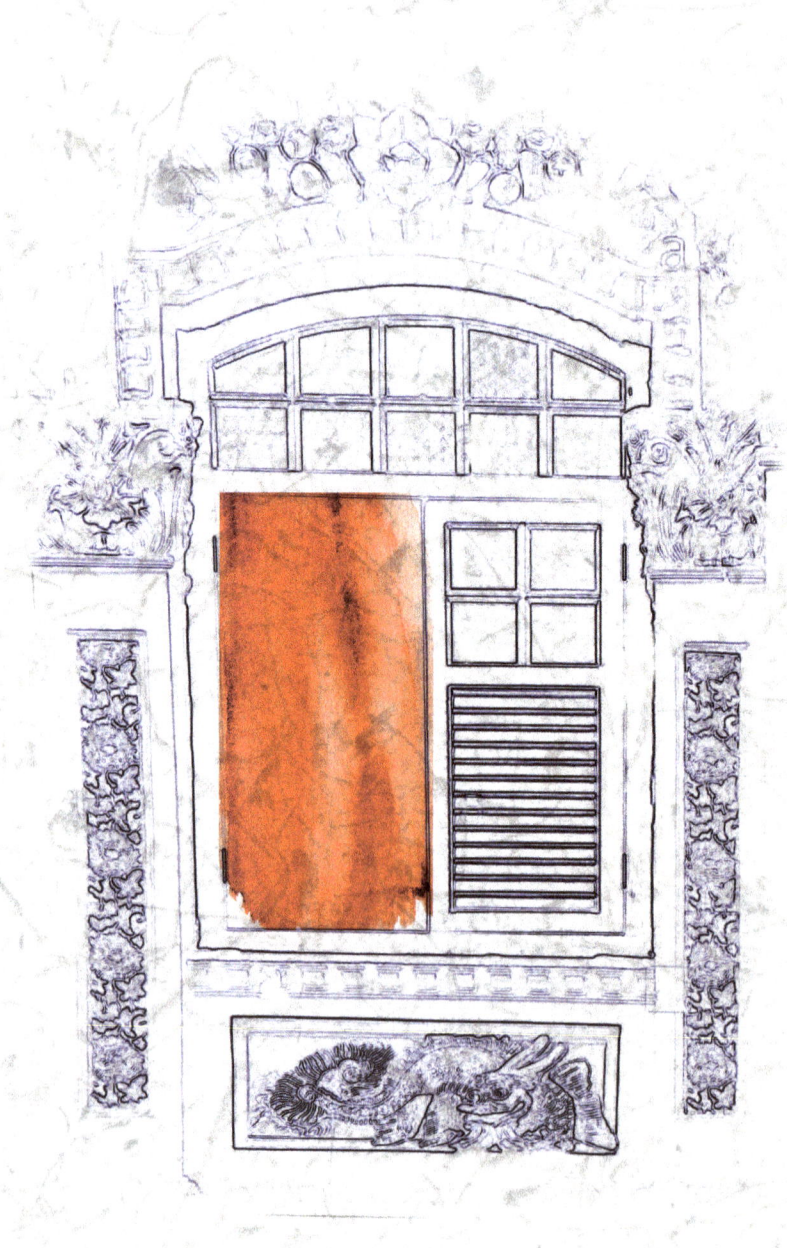

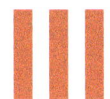

> *Art doesn't come from a natural impulse,
> but from calculated artifice*
>
> — *Sylvère Lotringer*

I would like to begin right away by excusing myself because I know very little of what I am about to attempt to speak on, very little of what I write.

This perhaps, being an excuse that comes a little too late. After all, I have already begun, at least in terms of words, scribbles, marks, remarks.

Not that we can quite know when we ever actually begin.

Or, where a line even starts.

Perhaps then, I should have begun by asking to begin again. For, one might have already begun at the moment when, in the very instant, one has — when I had — agreed to write on, speak about, the possibility of *art as resistance*, the moment I responded to a call from my friend, Mohan Dutta — patched to a line from him, connected a line to his kind invitation — to attend to a relation that I know precious little about.

Which is not a disavowal of what I am writing, what I am saying, about to say.

Far from it.

For, unlike Martin Heidegger, I am not about to deny that picking up a call — even a call that one might not have necessarily wanted, had not called for, as it were — that attending to a call, does not already entail a response. A disavowal that he declared, perhaps performed, even staged, when he refused responsibility for responding to a call from the *Sturmabteilung*; dismissing his role, saying: « someone from the top command of the Storm Trooper University Bureau, SA section leader Baumann called me up. He demanded … »

Not a: I picked up the phone, answered the call.

But a: it wasn't my choice, not even of my doing — after all, « he demanded ».

Which translates to: how could I not do so, *how could I even say no*.

Which is also an attempt at transposing genres: that, it is not so much a call but a *summons*: that, this was no ordinary sound made from a distance — he was a Storm Trooper, a figure from, and of, authority; it was *daddy calling me …*

which was strange response; particularly since it was coming from someone who had devoted his thinking to events, to possibilities, to the call of otherness.

For, why do some calls matter, and why do others not; and is it ever possible to dismiss a call that one has answered? Is it even possible to constitute it as a call — or even a summons — if it were not answered?

And, as my dear teacher, Avital Ronell, reminds us in *The Telephone Book*, « if Heidegger was there to receive the SA call, it is because he first had to accept the *Be-ruf*, or position, from which that ordering call could be picked up, that of rector, a position he held from 1933 to 1934 ». Thus, this call « takes place within a context of a prior call, though not in terms of a subject's desire but in those of an inescapable calling or vocation ». If Heidegger could not turn down daddy's call, it was because he had first accepted the call — the *ruf* — to be a son. For, the very condition of its possibility as a call is that one answers, even if that answer were to turn away, to reject, to refuse the content of the call; the call itself is always already answered at the very moment when one recognises it as a call. And more precisely — since one can never know if the call was even intended for one — by recognising its status as a call, one has already adopted it for oneself; and in doing so, opened oneself to its effects, to being affected by the call; by doing so, it is authorised as a call.

And, as Werner Hamacher, dear dear Werner, tries never to let us forget: to even constitute something as a call, one has to acknowledge that it comes from beyond. Perhaps, more importantly, there is absolutely no reason to assume that it was meant for you, otherwise there were no need to answer it, to respond to it — thus, in picking up a call, one always already runs the risk of answering a call that was never even sent to one. Which also means that to pick up a call is not only to recognise it as a call but to always already assume it for oneself.

Even if the call had picked one …not that there is any way of ever knowing so.

Which is not to say that one necessarily — or ever — knows what one picks up, has picked up, upon picking up the call. For, to assume it for oneself always also means that one runs the risk of not only assuming that one has the right to pick up, but that one has quite possibly made the assumption that it is a call.

> *Language is essentially discrete: what it expresses can always also be used as an instrument of encryption, a means of dissembling, disfiguring, or lying. Since, however, it constitutes all oppositions in the first place, it can belong to none of them, neither to concealment nor disclosure, neither publicity nor privacy and its idiosyncrasies.*
>
> — *Werner Hamacher*

Where, what is quite possibly being *calculated* is whether there had been, whether there even is, a call.

Where, one might be doing nothing other than *hearing voices in one's head.*

And where, one might well be writing that very call — where all I might be doing is inscribing Mohan's call — that is heard, that is thought to have been heard, into existence.

All whilst trying never to forget Hélène Cixous', dear dear Hélène's, reminder that, « when I write, it's everything that we don't know we can be that is written out of me, without exclusions, without stipulation, and everything we will be calls us to the unflagging, intoxicating, unappeasable search for love ».

Or, as I might say, have said elsewhere,
when I write I am always already *writing death*.

And where, even when, even in, writing death, language
remains discrete — and keeps its secrets.

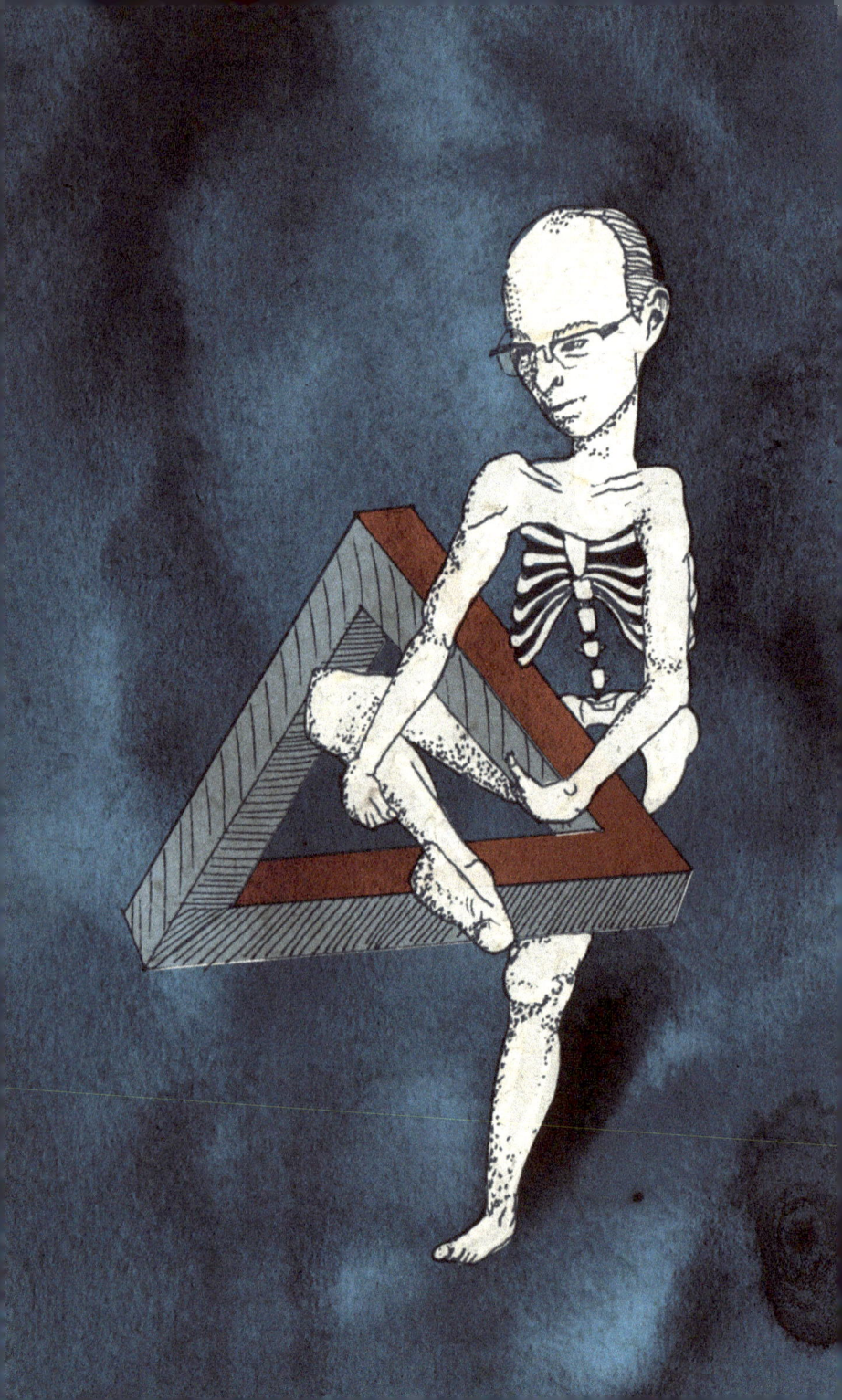

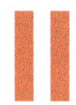

Every translation signifies the space-between, the gap, the historical chasm or the repression of history; translation is the most cautious form of communication since there is always the inherent admission of a certain departure and an uncertain arrival.

— *Hubertus von Amelunxen*

I would like to begin right away by excusing myself because I know very little of what I am about to attempt to write on, very little of what I write.

Even as this might be
an excuse that perhaps comes too late:
for, even as I am making it, it is already made, can only be made, in writing. Which is not to say that I am attempting to disavow what I have written, what I will write, but that perhaps all writing lies in excusing — in requesting a pardon, in asking for forgiveness.

Here I should recall why we confess to God who knows, our confitemur Deo scienti, why we only truly confess ourselves to God-who-knows because He knows it is not a question of knowing; and on condition: on condition there is no other witness than God-who-knows, on condition we make our confession to no one other than God, therefore to No One, to God-who-knows-as-likewise-He-does-not-know, to God the Ear for my word, God as my very own Ear into which, out of my silence, I thrust my avowal, aloud, in order to hear myself and (not) be heard by anyone else (other than God).

—*Hélène Cixous*

Bearing in mind — for, this should always be a burden on one — that one can only confess to one, to another, who already knows. For, confession is not a matter of knowledge: one confesses as if the other already knows of the transgression. Whether this is true — both the confession and the transgression — is beside the point: otherwise, it is only a matter of revealing, of telling. Confession lies in asking: regardless of whether the other knows if (s)he has been wronged — quite possibly even if either the request, or the matter of being wronged, is a lie.

And, this is why confessions can only be a rite, can only take place through rituals: for, it is not so much a matter of what is being confessed, but the fact that a confession takes place, that one has confessed. Thus, confessions are strictly speaking meaningless: it is not their signification that matters, but the significance of their occurrence.

Where perhaps, what is being staged — somewhat calculated in its performance — is the very confession itself: for, one should also try not to forget that a confession is only one *when it is seen* as a confession by the one whom one confesses to, when it is recognised as one.

So perhaps, what is being calculated, if one can call it that, but certainly being set up — keeping in mind that *theoria* always already invokes, brings with it, echoes of staging, setting up, performing, putting up in front of others — what is being put on, is the very conversation between the one who reads, the one who writes, and the texts. After all, one should try not to forget that this might well be why Plato calls them *dialogues*.

For, conversation always already — or, at least, should — entail turning around with (*conversare*), perhaps even *dancing with*, another, even if the other is oneself. And even at points of disagreement, divergence, even at points of potential combat (*versus*), the other and one are still in relation, still with each other (*con-*): where perhaps what is being staged is the very possibility of the relationship itself.

And where, what is being calculated — for, even as relationships (between one and a work, one and another, a work and one) might well begin as accidents, as chance encounters, perhaps even events, maintaining them, keeping them alive as possibilities, as it were, requires time, effort, work even — what is being accounted for, is the very possibility of this dance.

Especially if one is attempting to write in response with, as a response to: for, even as I attempt to respond to works, to thoughts, ideas, texts, calls, in all of their possibilities, one can — I can — never be certain if I am writing on, writing about, or writing over, these very works. Even worse: all of my words are, my writing is, haunted by the possibility that all I am doing is making the calls, texts, ideas, thoughts, works, say what I want them to say; bringing them forth in order that they, conjuring them such that they, speak for me;

prosopopoeia

So perhaps:
not just that each writing (*écriture*) is writhing in the possibility that it is saying something other than it should, is struggling with the fact that it is speaking over, silencing, what it is attempting to speak for, but that in order for writing to maintain a certain responsibility, to maintain the possibility that it is responding, it would have to always also be erasing what it writes.

Where each scribble, *scribere*, not only scratches into, stains — paints — the surface on which it is writing, but always also scratches out, tears, opens, runs the possibility of wounding, tearing as it is tearing, crying out (*cri*).

Where perhaps, every moment of trying to know, to grasp, to comprehend, to take into one's hand, *prendre* — every attempt to answer, to respond, to attend to a call — is to always already render it dead. But where perhaps, it is love, *philia*, in its unknowability — in its refusal to claim the other for itself — which maintains the space for life.

Where, love is quite possibly another name for a relation to the possibility of another — a relation where both the other and one remain wholly other to each other.

Where, all that the one who writes can perhaps say is — without knowing either what (s)he says, nor even who the I who writes is —

> *I love you: I work at understanding you to the point of not understanding you, and there, standing in a wind, I don't understand you. Not understanding in a way of holding myself in front and of letting come. Transverbal, transintellectual relationship, this loving the other in submission to the mystery. (It's accepting, not knowing, forefeeling, feeling with the heart.) I'm speaking in favour of non-recognition, not of mistaken cognition. I'm speaking of closeness, without any familiarity.*

always already — and perhaps only possible — in the words of another, the other.

—*Hélène Cixous*

Keeping in mind the possibility that art is the very movement — *trans-* — of what is brought forth through craft, by *tekhnē*, into something else, something other than itself. Not that the one who makes it is any different — even if (s)he might never quite remain the same after. Even though, perhaps precisely because, there is no guarantee that (s)he might ever be able to do so again, repeat it, make it again; nor even if (s)he might recognise the possibility of art in what (s)he has crafted.

Where perhaps, *what is art* and *what is craft* might well be the same, but at the same time, *same same but different*.

Where, it is not just that difference lies within sameness, nor merely that there is sameness in differences, but that what is same is always already different — for, the very notion of same is a relation, and in relation lies difference.

Where, in its relation to craft, art might always be *un pas au-delà*.

Thus, quite possibly unseen, un-seeable — and where, the one who sees the art in any moment of craft might well be the only one who sees it, might well be hearing what (s)he thinks is a call from and of the work, might well be hearing only what (s)he hears. For, all she can do is to be in relation with the work; and more precisely, a relation of
« not understanding in a way of holding myself in front and of letting come ».

Which is not to say that art is antithetical to knowing, to knowledge, nor its antonym: but that it is a knowing that does not know, *un savoir qui ne voit pas*.

Which might well be why her owl only flies in the twilight — for, the goddess always knew that the transformation from *tekhnē* to art happens due to the movement of the world. Not that one sees the world differently — nothing that banal — but when there is a gap between the object and what is seen. When a chair is both a chair, in all its usefulness, its so-called purpose, but at the same time not-quite-just-a-chair; where the purposefulness of crafting this chair is somehow *just slightly beyond* its purpose: just slightly beyond — this gap — being nothing other than not just *un pas au-delà*, but also another name for the *chair-ness* of the chair.

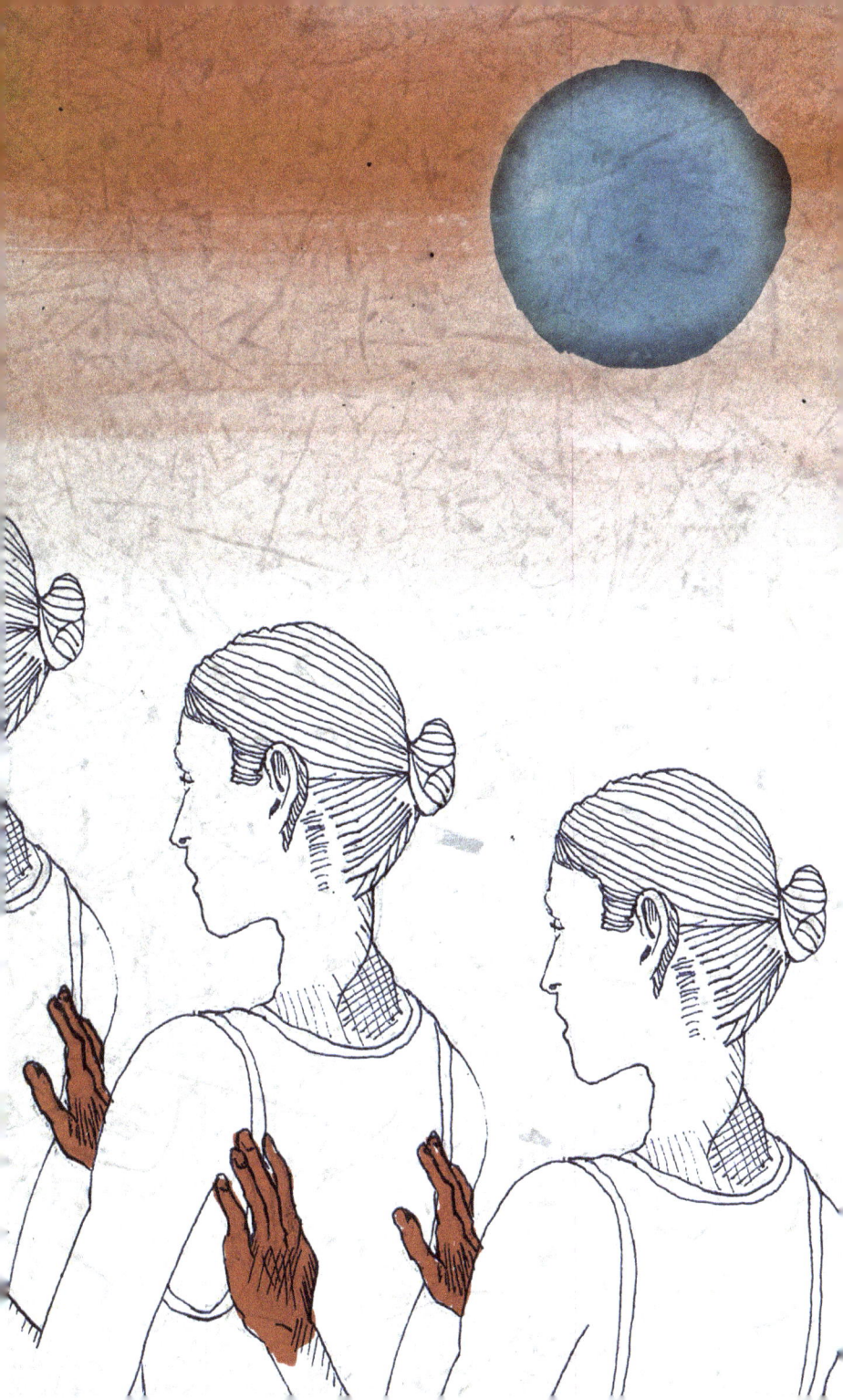

art:

or, another name for
a transcendence that is not transcendental,
an *immanent transcendence*.

Which also means that it might well be a moment that escapes one — perhaps, not because one did not experience it, nor that this experience did not register with one, but that it is quite possibly an instance that writes itself into us in the very instant that it is scratched out of us.

A moment which is *read*.

A particular approach to reading that came to me in a lunch conversation with Werner Hamacher — a moment of speech that is recalled, that continually calls out to me, now in script, inscribed; but since only ever heard by me, might also never have been heard, that possibly might never quite have happened.

I see myself first and foremost as a reader: reading being understood as the relation to an other that occurs prior to any semantic or formal identification, and therefore prior to any attempt at assimilating what is being read to the one who reads. As neither an act or rule-governed operation, reading needs to be thought as an event of an encounter with an other—and more precisely an other which is not the other as identified by the reader, but heterogeneous in relation to any identifying determination. Thus, a pre-relational relationality where what the reader encounters may only be encountered before any phenomenon; hence a non-phenomenal event or even the event of undoing all phenomenality.

—*Jeremy Fernando*

Not that what is remembered, recalled, and what is forgotten are antonymous: for, one should try not to forget that forgetting has no object. Thus, not only can one never quite know what one has forgotten, but that there is no reason that each memory, each act of remembering, might not bring with it, might not be inscribed with, forgetting.

Where, memory is always already potentially elliptical … all whilst trying to remember that one can only write what one knows, what one thinks one knows; thus, what one recalls.

Ellipsis is the rhetorical equivalent of writing: it depletes, or de-completes, the whole so as to make conceptual totalities possible. And yet every conceivable whole achieved on the basis of ellipsis is stamped with the mark of the original loss. Ellipsis eclipses (itself). It is the figure of figuration: the area no figure contains.

—*Werner Hamacher*

Keeping in mind that an ellipsis suggests that there is either something more, or something less, in a sentence — it can suggest more to be added, or a retraction … or perhaps, a space, a gap, for something. Thus, it marks, it is the mark of, an unknown — and perhaps always unknowable — effect.

And, since forgetting can occur at any time, and place, there is then no reason why each act of remembering (that is recalled in, and by, the sentence) might not always already bring with it the possibility of forgetting.

That, regardless of whether one sees an ellipsis, every sentence might always already be elliptical.

And, where writing itself might bring with it what the one who writes might well have forgotten …

> … to be read —
> even as reading is always also potentially a re-writing,
> a writing over, perhaps even an effacement of this very
> forgetting itself.

And since beauty is of the order of the whole, the complete, this also means that it, like every « conceivable whole », is « stamped with the mark of the original loss » … is quite possibly elliptical.

And where art — allowing all echoes of Immanuel Kant and *the sublime* to haunt us here — which is a possible opening, a potential rupture, *peut-être même un éclat*, is quite possibly *beauty without being beautiful*, an experience of beauty without quite being able to call it beautiful, without subsuming it under any prior conception of the beautiful; where beauty remains a name naming quite possibly nothing other than an *aisthesis* which overwhelms us.

Where, art is perhaps nothing other than another name for *forgetting* itself …

Beauty will be amnesiac or, will not be at all.

—*Sylvère Lotringer*

The work of art is not an instrument of communication. The work of art has nothing to do with communication. The work of art strictly does not contain the least bit of information. To the contrary, there is a fundamental affinity between the work of art and the act of resistance. There, yes. It has something to do with information and communication as acts of resistance. What is this mysterious relation between a work of art and an act of resistance when men who resist have neither the time nor sometimes the necessary culture to have the least relation to art?

I don't know.

—Gilles Deleuze

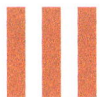

Keeping in mind that the moment a work informs, it lies within an established system — and replicates not only itself within the confines, boundaries, rules, laws, of said system, but the very structures of power that bring forth that very system. For, a piece of information — a « grouping of order-words » within a « controlled system », « used in a given society » — is always also composed of words that order us, group one into an *us*.

Which is precisely how communication — through *les communiqués* — shapes one into behaving as part of, playing an appropriate role in, a society of control.

But what if the work is housed, is enframed —
behind glass, perhaps in a museum. For, the moment the muses are housed, encased, are placed within an *oikos*, they are also withdrawn from the polis, from the public. They are made private — never forgetting that to be private is also to

be made voiceless; to be excluded from citizenry; to be the one that cannot learn; to be an *idiotes*.

Much like when they are taken (*prendre*) by, taken into, one's grasp — placed under one's conception, one's comprehension.

For, it should weigh on one's mind that the moment one attempts to attend to it, to address it, write about it, speak on it — even if one is attempting to open oneself to possibilities, to potentialities — one is not only tempted to know, to understand, to make sense of the work, one has no choice but to, if only momentarily, bring it under one's own conceptions, framework; *en bref*, in attending to, in picking up, its call, the call of the work, one always already tames it, turns it into information.

And thus, perhaps unintentionally, rather inadvertently, the very moment of response might well be the instant when the potential « acts of resistance » in and of the work are already muted.

After all, the road to hell is often paved with good intentions.

Trying also never to forget that every time one writes about something, one not only writes it, but also writes its context, into existence — recontextualing it, if one is feeling generous with oneself; but really decontextualising into and — with a new framing that has little, maybe even nothing at all, to do with it.

Keeping in mind that, to frame is always also to *potentially accuse* someone of something that (s)he might not have done.

frame

is art, art, without the frame?

After all, a painting of sunflowers on a wall is graffiti; with(in) a frame it is — or, at least, is potentially called — art. Where, it only has a name — one might even say it is called to its name — within those walls.

Which opens another question: *is it only art when it has a name?* And, perhaps more importantly, *whose name?*: that of the work, or that of the one who signs on the work?

Both of which — the frame and the name — are questions of context: of situation; of materiality. Which suggests that any consideration of art — even if we take art to mean *the movement from a work made through craft, brought forth through tekhnē, to something beyond it* — cannot be divorced from its material reality.

support

Does the frame support the work, or the work support the frame?

Can there even be one without the other?

After all, to *call* it, to *name* it as, *work* is to enframe it: where the name is quite possibly the frame, whilst, at the same time, is called into being a name by the very framing of the work, is only the name of the work as it is framed from the work itself. Where, it is nothing other than its framing that names it as either work or frame— the threshold between the two being not only porous, but somewhat indiscernible.

To pass a sentence on her, him, it.
Branding it, him, her,
with letters, thoughts, words.

>Enframing the work
>— and perhaps even her maker —
>in a cenotaph.

Peut-être,
comme moi,
comme je fais,
comme je n'ai pas d'autre choix que de faire.

Which also means: that even as art may be *un pas au-delà*,
this is a step beyond work that is at the same time not
beyond, and perhaps never beyond, work.

But, as Jean-Christophe Bailly teaches us,
« *pour moi, le doute est la base du métier d'écrivain* ».

>For him,
>but also for me.

Which might be why,
I can never quite be sure of what I say …

Art is what resists,
even if it is not
the only thing that
resists.

—*Gilles Deleuze*

Much like how the potentiality of
a work of art perhaps lies in the
possibility that the « affinity » between
the work of art and an act of resistance
is a « mysterious relation ». Where it
can be glimpsed, sensed even, but that
the exact relationship remains beyond
one, outside the realm of cognition, where — in attempting
to speak of that relationship — one can perhaps only say,

I don't know.

All whilst trying not to forget that true mysteries have the power — an unknown power — to make us tremble.

For, all that one can know is that one encounters a mystery — nothing more, and infinitely nothing less.

An encounter:
where what one encounters « may only be encountered before any phenomenon; hence a non-phenomenal event or even the event of the undoing of all phenomenality ».

> Where all one might be able to say is
> — and even this remains uncertain —
> is that there might have been an encounter.

Perhaps here, it is the notion of *possibility*, of *potentiality*, that we have to momentarily turn our attention to; keeping in mind that potentiality is not merely a phase preceding actuality. Which is not to say that nothing will happen; not only can we not quite be sure of that, if it were so, it would no longer be a potential. Nor it is — as Giorgio Agamben likes to say — a « potential-to-be and a potential-not-to-be ». For, if that were so, the « not-to-be » would lie beyond potentiality. And, whilst there is something that quite possibly escapes potential, this is a beyond that is not outside the realm of potentiality, but within it — *un pas au-delà*.

Thus, potentiality — as Werner once said to me — is the *potential-to-be* and an *impotentiality not-to-be*, a potentiality that negates itself as a negation, but still shimmers there, as a possibility.

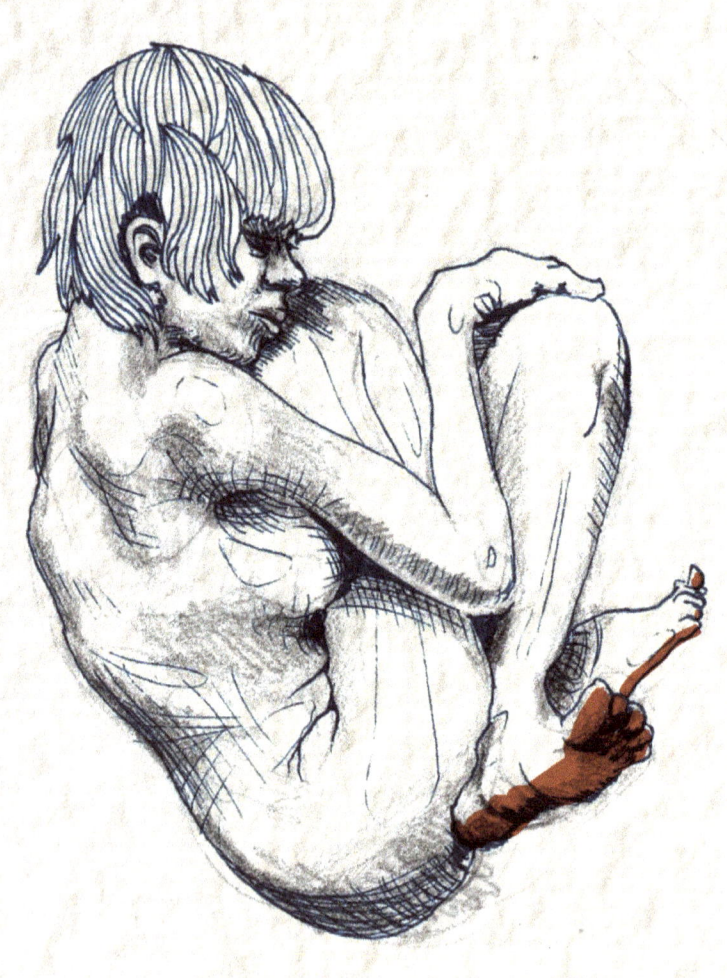

Which then brings with it a question of *not only what one can know*, but — perhaps more pertinently — *if one can even know what one cannot know*. And, at this point, it might be helpful to turn to a most unusual, a terribly unlikely, source for thought, for questions about knowing, about truth even — one Donald Rumsfeld. In particular, his statement in February 2002, during a news briefing by the United States Department of Defense, when he quipped, « but the truth is, there are things we know, and we know we know them — the *known knowns*. There are things we know that we don't know — the *known unknowns*. And there are *unknown unknowns*; the things we do not yet know that we do not know ». For, perhaps unbeknownst to him, Rumsfeld had stumbled upon a key problem of knowing and knowledge; that of the relationship between the object of inquiry and the subject's awareness of the existence of that object. In his first scenario — the « known knowns » — the subject is both aware of the object and has a cognitive understanding of it. In the case of the « known unknowns », the subject is aware of her lack of cognitive understanding of the object. It is more interesting in the case of the « unknown unknowns » : here, the subject is unaware of the fact that (s)he lacks a cognitive understanding — this would be the case of an absolute lack of knowledge. Unfortunately for Rumsfeld — as one of my dear teachers, Slavoj Žižek, has shown us — the problem, amongst many other problems, with Donald Rumsfeld is that he did not quite go far enough: for, he missed the fourth variation, that of the *unknown knowns*. In this iteration, the subject is unaware of the fact that (s)he knows something — where, there is an indeterminability of knowledge. Which means that, one — let alone the subject herself — is never able to determine whether (s)he knows or does not know something. However, just because (s)he is unaware of something does not mean it has no effects on her: for, even as (s)he might be completely blind to it, it can quite possibly affect her.

> *Trauma structures us; so hold on to it.*
>
> —*Avital Ronell*

For, an *unknown known* is somewhat akin to a traumatic event; in which something occurs to one, but where one is unable to comprehend it, understand it, or even realise that it might have taken place, let alone how and why it might have taken hold of, taken over, one. And where, the effects take the form of symptoms — *traces* that are written on, inscribed into, one's body. And where all attempts to attend to these traces take the form of, can only happen through, readings; attempt to read these marks, to see what these remarks leave us as notes. For, even if a *substitute formation* is created, as Freud might say — keeping in mind that this is a rewriting, a writing over — and the analysand goes on to believe that the 'cause' of their symptoms is found, this is of the order of faith rather than knowledge.

Where, even as « trauma structures us », the way in which it does so quite possibly remains a mystery — and not only might what one holds on to remained veiled from one, so to is its possible *hold on one*.

And here, one should keep in mind that this inherent blindness is not exclusive to trauma: in fact, it is the very nature of — if one can call anything that one attempts to conceive of natural — is what is innate to, all events. For, since they are only cognitised — or brought to bear under reason — after their occurrence, this would be the creation of that very same *substitute formation*: where, all one is doing is, all one can do is to be, writing the very attempt at understanding into place. Where, not only is one blind to any event, every event is traumatic: for, one knows not of the event as such; and all one can sense, might be able to *feel*, are its traces, how it has traced itself onto, written itself into, one.

Much like art.

Which might be why, as Jean Baudrillard never stops reminding us, « the poem lacks nothing: any commentary makes it worse. Not only does it lack nothing, but it makes any other discourse look superfluous ».

For, even as we read a poem, even as we attempt to respond to it — write onto, write over, it even — *the poem keeps its secrets.*

Bearing in mind that secrets lie not so much in their content, but in their form as secret. Where, the power of a secret, any secret, is not in its signification but lies in its significance. Which suggests that not only can a secret be staring one in the face — be hiding in plain view, as it were — but, more importantly, that to know something is a secret, one must also be able to see it for something other than its semantic meaning.

> Things keep their secrets.
>
> —*Heraclitus*

For *what it is not.*

Which is not to say that one can ever quite know what is not: all one can do is to recognise that it is not — a negation which does not negate itself into a known, into what is known, but which remains, which shimmers in its very negation.

Which means that all one can do is to recognise its significance: nothing more, and infinitely nothing less.

Which also means that:
its significance — even as one recognises it as significant —
has naught to do with one.

> Which might well be why it is possible for The Mole,
> our friend Christophe who lives down the road from us in
> South Park, to say,
> *'though I die, la resistance lives on.*

And where there is quite possibly no artist —
only the ones who make through their craft; and perhaps
gestures of the possibility of, *whispers* from the possibility
called, art.

Much like literature.
Keeping in mind that literature is always already a reading
(*lit*) of what is in erasure, of what deletes (*rature*), is erasing
itself (*se raturer*), as it is being read, or even, what is constantly
under *erasure* (*sous rature*) — precisely by being aware of the
fact that it is written, that it is being told.

Unlike propaganda, which — as Jonas Staal teaches us —
« is about shaping our environment, engineering our reality ».
For, he continues, « propaganda is the performance of
power ».

Literature, on the other hand, which foregrounds the fact
that it is written — and has to be read — gives its hand away:
stages the fact that it is a *calculated artifice* which has *absolutely
nothing* to do with our reality, our environment, the world in
which we live.

Which is why literature itself is fundamentally useless.

And this is precisely why those in power have always been fearful of it.

Here, one should try not to forget that the first to be shot are always poets and writers. Not because they actually do anything, but that precisely by doing nothing they give — allowing all echoes of gift to resound — they open, the space for us to imagine something else, something other. And by entwining literature with use, all that is done is to tie it down, enchain it, to the state.

Ironically, those who claim to love literature are the ones who have done the most violence to it. One can hear this in complaints from those who write, avid readers, ones who teach: these include claims such as *we should be taken more seriously; I wish people would stop saying that we only read story books; we are transmitting important life skills to our students* — attempts at, gestures towards, *gravitas*.

But, what else is literature but the reading of stories. Which is not to say that stories are only found in books. However, what is crucial is the love for stories: and this is learned, developed, nurtured, through an attention towards, alongside a love of, and for, books. And here, one should tune in to the echoes of both *book* and *learning* that resonate in literature (from the Old English *boccræft*).

And once we open the register of learning, we should also not forget the accompanying dossiers of *mimesis*, repetition, habit, and *habitus*. For, as my dear teacher, my dear friend, Neil Murphy might say: « show me what you read and I'll tell you who you are ».

For, we are always already in relation with what we read: where, whenever one reads, one has to first open oneself to the possibility of reading, open oneself to reading itself;

without necessarily — quite possibly, without ever — knowing what reading even is.

Thus, to claim that literature has a use is to diminish it, to enslave it to value, production, logic, ratio, reason. Which is to do nothing other than to attempt to erase literature.

Which is not to say that literature has no effect on us.

But that is not its point.
For, what affects us only happens after, or perhaps during, the encounter with the text; and this is not where literature as such lies. For, literature lies in *letters* (*littera*); and like all writing, it is of the order of death.

Which means that:
to love literature is to be *in love with* the dead.

Necrophilia.

All whilst holding onto Alain Badiou's beautiful reminder that to love is to be in a relation that « encompasses the experience of the possible transition from the pure randomness of chance to a state that has universal value ». Which is not to diminish « pure randomness » ; on the contrary, the very possibility of love rests on it, hinges on *taking a chance*.

And the gamble that is taken each time one picks up a book, the risk one runs in attempting to attend to a text, is the possibility of *falling* — along with all the potential disasters this entails — in love.

Thus, the very stake in literature is one's self.

And, if writing is of the order of death,
reading is, quite possibly then, an openness to the possibility of resurrection.

And more than that, if literature is a love of the dead, opening oneself to death is an openness to the unknown, and potentially always unknowable. Which may be why Milan Kundera calls it the *unbearable lightness of being*: where, it is the refusal to be grounded, to be pinned down, known, that is unbearable, that continually provokes us, challenges us, quite possibly scares us, perhaps even tears us apart.

It is perhaps symptomatic that there is often a *crisis* in literature at the moments when states are obsessed with concocting an identity. For, if reading literature is about love for the unknown, is about possibilities, it is, thus, of the order of difference rather than identification, sameness.

In other words, literature is always anti-stasis, anti-state. More than that, it is always also a challenge to the self, to our selves: it is a call to attend to the possibility of another, of something that is more important than oneself, almost certainly beyond one's self.

And like any call, it might well lead us to dash ourselves on the rocks.

Herein lies its danger.

And its beauty.

> ...when we lose someone, we do not always know what it is in that person that has been lost. So when one loses, one is also faced with something enigmatic: something is hiding in the loss, something is lost within the recesses of loss. If mourning involves knowing what one has lost (and melancholia originally meant, to a certain extent, not knowing), then mourning would be maintained by its enigmatic dimension, by the experience of not knowing incited by losing what we cannot fully fathom...
>
> —*Judith Butler*

Where, it is quite possible that the *art* in literature lies precisely in its moment of beauty — thus, always already *stamped with the mark of an original loss* — in its erasure; in *what it is not*, not that *what is* and *what is not* are antonyms, but that they are perhaps in an elliptical relationship ...

Where, it is the ellipsis that opens the relation, the very possibility of a conversation between. At the same time, the two or more in that relation are also never exactly at the same point, in the same place: after all, as Jean-Luc Nancy tries to never let us forget, « it is space that is first needed for touch » : without the gap between, not only is touch unnecessary, it is also impossible, for the other has been completely effaced by one.

Where, it is the ellipsis that also ensures that it is never quite possible to claim complete knowledge, to have any *metaphysical certainty*, as Nietzsche might say, that one knows ... for, even as it bridges, brings closer, opens the possibility of touching, it also ensures that the two or more in relation, in that relationship, are apart whilst being a part of, remain wholly other to each other.

> *Art lies in the gap between the frame and the viewer.*
>
> —*Slavoj Žižek*

Where *ellipsis* is quite possibly
nothing other than another name for *art*.

And where, all one can do is attempt to approach this gap …
and open oneself to its possibilities … without claiming to
know, without any assurance that one will ever know … like
an *amateur*, like one who is open to the possibility of being in
love (*amore*).

> There is a whole art in unfurling a body of thought in such a way that one ends up passing it by without seeing it. This is the opposite of discourse, which lays out its findings and arguments and sentences itself to house arrest within the precincts of its own conclusions.
>
> —*Jean Baudrillard*

And where — if one is attempting a relation of *non-recognition* with the work, a relation of *closeness without any familiarity* — what one is doing is nothing other than *resisting art* …

… in the very sense of resisting the call …

not so much from the work — (art does not call) — but from attempts to enframe it, from the people who attempt to frame it.

And where, all that one can *feel* — whilst *holding in front and letting come* — is that one is in a mysterious relation with the work.

But thankfully, even as we are resisting art, *art resists us*, and is what remains — resisting resistance itself …

… shimmering in a *non-negative negation* … in all of its potentiality … as a possibility …

… even when one is attempting to write about, speak on, it.

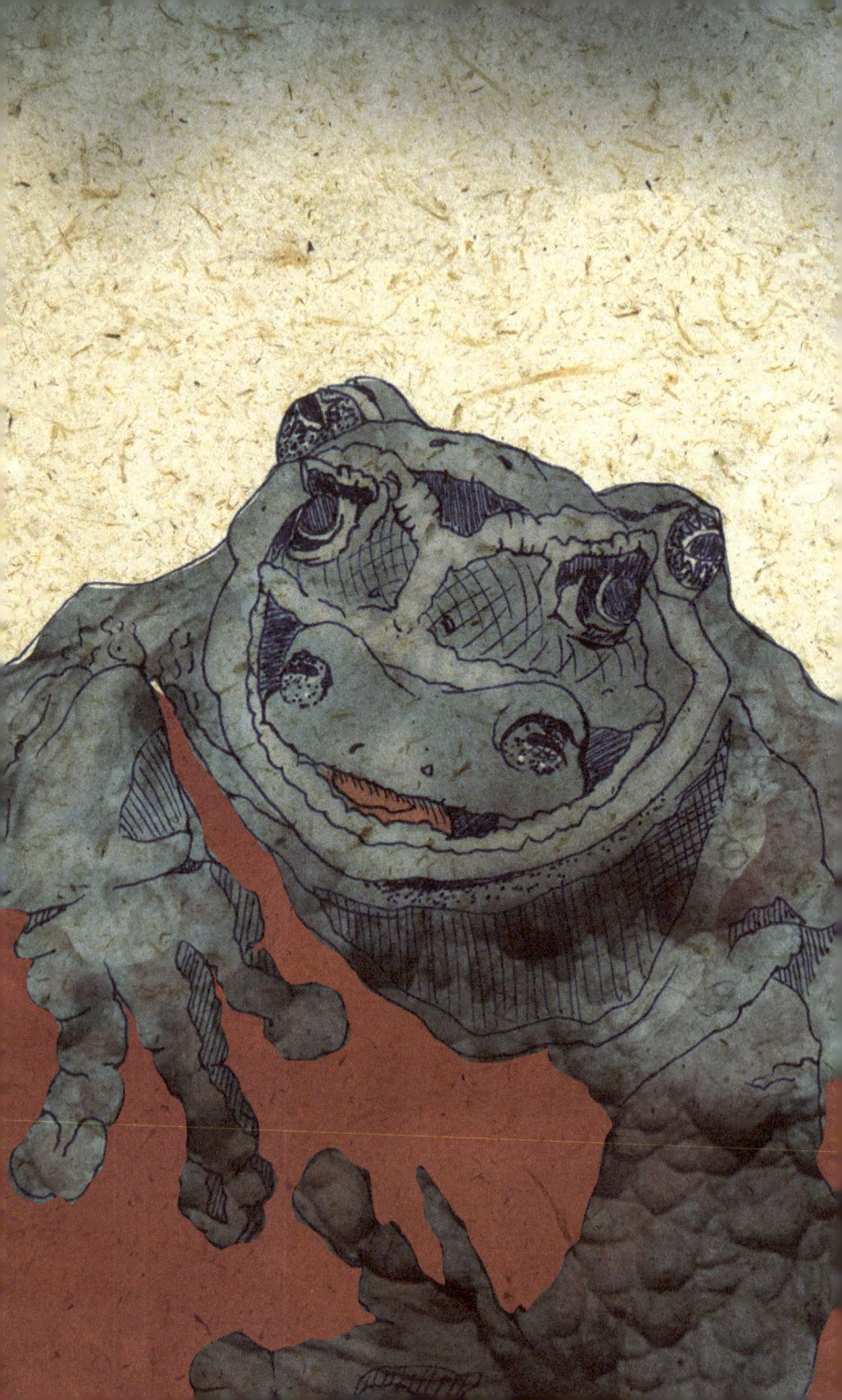

independent art

To speak of the independence of some thing is to neglect its dependency. For, to speak of any thing is to open its relationality to, its relationship with, another.

Which makes the term *independent art* a strange one — and brings with it the question, independent *of* what?

Or: independence *from* what?

Certainly, one of the hopes of most artisans is for their work to be free from external pressures — most commonly, commerce. Which is perhaps why many choose to apply for grants; or to hold multiple jobs in order to free themselves, give themselves the freedom, to make the work that they want to. However, this also means that they are either obliged, bonded, bound — explicitly or otherwise — to whomever is funding them; or beholden to a lack of time. And here, one should not forget that making work is always bodily, entails the body — and a body that is tired, that is drained, a body whose energy has been sucked up by labour, is one that is possibly already a shell without a ghost, *un corps sans esprit*, by the time one attempts to make one's work.

Where, what emerges from one is quite possibly the product of labour and time — and *not* work; in the precise sense that what emerges is alienated from the one who makes it; where what emerges is not brought forth with and through the self.

Moreover, the fact that work is material — comes into being in, and through, materiality — suggests that it is always already indivorceable from exchangeability. For, even if the artisan did not pay for the said materials, the fact that they are now utilised for the work, and not for another purpose, suggests it has an exchange value. Where, the withdrawal of the materials from circulation entails a certain cost — an opportunity cost, if you prefer.

Here, I am in agreement with Sylvère Lotringer and Jean Baudrillard, both of whom argue that *use-value* is a misnomer: for, the value of something lies in it being exchanged, in its exchangeability; is premised on, can only be generated through, exchange.

Thus, *exchange-value* is tautological.

One might even say that the term *use-value* attempts to maintain the notion that materiality has an inherent value, that there is a 'proper use' for something — and in that way, is an attempt to hold on to the fantasy of a means of production where exchange is not always abstract; where we are not alienated, always already separated, from that production. And stave-off the fact that our relationship with materials, with the world, with any and every other — even if it involves production — is always already mired in exchange, in valuation, in consumption.

However, even as this is an important consideration, this does not address the notion of art itself: for, this flattens the difference(s) between work and art. For, surely not everything an artisan produces can be considered art.

So, let's begin again, start anew.

To begin to speak of *independent art*, one must first address the question: *what is art?*

A question haunted by another question, a dependent question: *is art, art, without the frame?* After all, a painting of sunflowers on a wall is graffiti; with(in) a frame it is — or, at least, is potentially called — art. It only has a name — one might even say it is called to its name — within those walls.

Which opens another question: *is it only art when it has a name?* And, perhaps more importantly, *whose name?*: that of the work, or that of the one who signs on the work?

Both of which — the frame and the name — are questions of context: of situation; once again, of materiality. Which suggests that any consideration of art — even if we take art to mean *the movement from a work made through craft, brought forth through tekhnē, to something beyond it* — cannot be divorced from its material reality.

Which also means that: even as art may be *un pas au-delà*, this is a step beyond work that is at the same time not, and perhaps never, beyond work.

Which then opens this question: *where* does the art lie? Perhaps in the presence of the original: for, who has not been genuinely moved by some work? But in this, the notion of names continues to be a spectre: for, is it the name that lends the aura to the work?

Would one be moved when standing in front of graffiti? It is certainly possible: after all, no one questions the power of Banksy's work. However, the moment one knows — or even thinks that — it is a Banksy, the link between the work and the name remains.

A more interesting question is perhaps then: *can a replica have an aura?* For, if the aura lies in the work itself, there is no reason why a perfect replication — whether or not this is possible is another question — should not. Which is a particularly pertinent question in the digital age: for, is there an un-original code to begin with?

Which is not to say that just because something is simulated it cannot move us; even if we know that it is so.

Far from it.

However, there is also little doubt that there is something different about an original: whether this is rational or not, or if it even has an explanation, is perhaps beside the point.

For perhaps, the notion of originality itself lies in it being called — named — as original: in its being *authored* as an origin (*auctor*).

Which opens the possibility that the originality of a work — the origin of a work — comes not so much from within but from elsewhere, from another. Keeping in mind that authority — for something, or someone, to become a figure of authority it, (s)he — must first be accepted by those who subjugate themselves under her, under it: this being a key distinction from power, which can be forced upon others — authority on the other hand is given, granted upon, another. And here, we should try not to forget that both *elsewhere* and *from another* are positions of relation — and, more importantly — are in themselves unknown, potentially unknowable, locations.

And perhaps, it is precisely the unlocatability of art that has to be considered.

Which opens a new register in the relationship between art and independence. For, if art is unlocatable, then surely it is always already independent: that would make the phrase *independent art*, tautological.

And, if unlocatable — and its aura can only be glimpsed as we stand before it — this suggests that the experience of art is singular.

Which also means that it is not — at least not necessarily — repeatable. And thus, non-exchangeable: for, exchangeability, no matter how symbolic, rests on there being at least a modicum of repeatability. Unless of course, one contends that what is being exchanged is the very simulation of exchangeability itself. In that case, one might then say that the term *art market* might well be tautological: for, the art — both by way of *artifice*; and, a *creation that is brought forth through a tekhnē* — is the market itself.

But perhaps, what remains interesting to us — to those of us who love art — is the fact that we *cannot* account for the origin of this aura. And since this is so, we also can never know whether, and when, we are in the presence of art until it affects us. And here, we should bear in mind the teachings of Plato through Socrates: that, for craft to move into the realm of — to transcend itself in becoming — art, the artisan needs a divine moment, needs to be affected by a whisper from the *daemon*. But, since this is a moment that comes from beyond, this suggests that it is exterior to the artisan's knowledge, self, perhaps even being: a moment in which (s)he might well know not what (s)he is doing — much like *love*, which always begins with a *fall*: not from some sort of grace, purity, wholeness, into some lesser, lower, fragment, but — rather — a moment of being struck by an unknown which has an effect on us; after which, all one can say is that *I was affected, moved*.

Which also means that to know that one has fallen in love, one has to first recognise it: that everything is the same — that the relation between the two, or more, is the same, that all in that relationship are still wholly other, both in themselves and in relation to the other(s) — but that something is also different: that in that very moment of love, there is always also, always already, the possibility of a *we*.

Perhaps then, in order to experience art, we might need that moment too; in which we see a work with new eyes: that in standing before that work, in experiencing the work, there is the possibility of a momentary *us*, a potential being *with* the work.

Even if this very work is the one that is made by us.
Even if it were brought forth by our very self.

And this might well be the very crux of *independent art*: that it is not so much that the art — or even the work — is independent from anything,

> but that the independence is of the one — (s)he — who is looking …

> … from her very self.

Where the possibility of art is the moment
in which one and the work is in communion.

> — where the moment of art
> is nothing other than another name for
> communism itself —

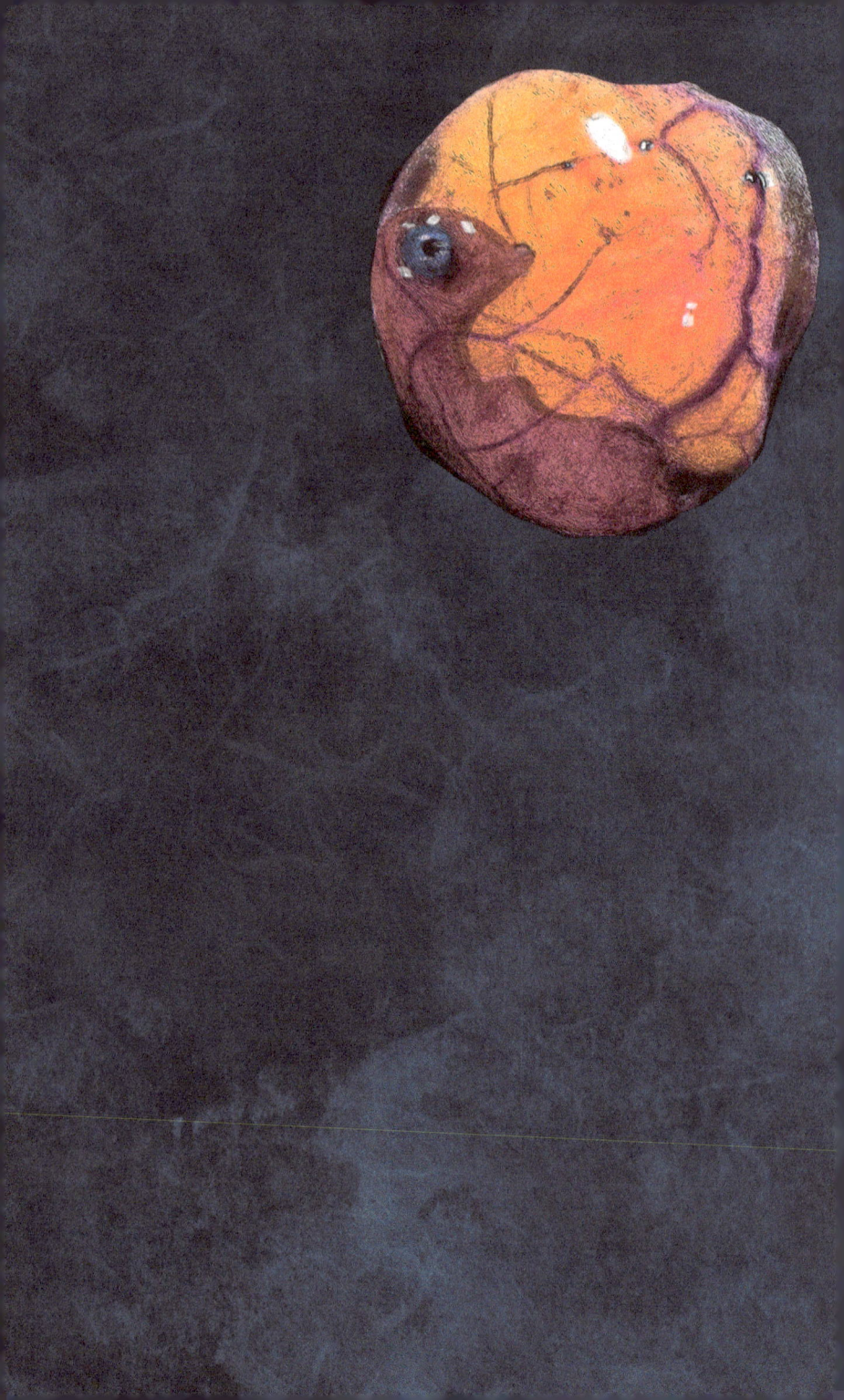

Contributors

Jeremy Fernando reads, and writes; and is the Jean Baudrillard Fellow at The European Graduate School. He works in the intersections of literature, philosophy, and the media; and his, more than twenty, books include *Reading Blindly*, *Living with Art*, *Writing Death*, and *in fidelity*. His writing has also been featured in magazines and journals such as *Arte al Límite*, *Berfrois*, *CTheory*, *Full Bleed*, *Qui Parle*, *TimeOut*, and *VICE*, amongst others; and has been translated into French, German, Italian, Japanese, Spanish, and Serbian. Exploring other media has led him to film, music, and the visual arts; and his work has been exhibited in Seoul, Vienna, Hong Kong, and Singapore. He is the general editor of the thematic magazine *One Imperative*; and is a Fellow of Tembusu College at the National University of Singapore.

Natalie Christian Tan is an illustrator, graphic designer, and occasional writer. She graduated from Yale-NUS College and was awarded the Outstanding Capstone Award for her thesis on selfies and the female image. Today, her visual work dwells heavily on reimagining archaic forms of art. Her work has been featured in publications from NUS Press, Harvard University Press, *Fox & Hedgehog*, and *Brack*. In her capacity as a writer, she has contributed pieces on Singaporean society to platforms like *Mynah Magazine*. Natalie hopes for the best, and that very much makes her ordinary.

A sampling of her work is available at http://nataliechristiantan.myportfolio.com.

www.ingramcontent.com/pod-product-compliance
Lightning Source LLC
Chambersburg PA
CBHW040522220526
45473CB00013B/2954